NO!

The art of saying No! with a clear conscience

Jesper Juul

Translated by Hayes van der Meer

AuthorHouse™
1663 Liberty Drive
Bloomington, IN 47403
www.authorhouse.com
Phone: 1-800-839-8640

© 2012 by Jesper Juul. All rights reserved.

No part of this book may be reproduced, stored in a retrieval system, or transmitted by any means without the written permission of the author.

www.jesperjuul.com
www.family-lab.com
www.artofsayingno.tv
www.familylab.com.au

Your Competent Child, published by Balboa Press

DVD Your Competent Child at www.textalk.se

English titles published by AuthorHouse:

Family Life
Family Time
Here I am! Who are you?

Published by AuthorHouse   07/20/2012

ISBN: 978-1-4685-7930-7 (sc)
ISBN: 978-1-4685-7931-4 (hc)
ISBN: 978-1-4685-7932-1 (e)

Any people depicted in stock imagery provided by Thinkstock are models, and such images are being used for illustrative purposes only.
Certain stock imagery © Thinkstock.

This book is printed on acid-free paper.

Because of the dynamic nature of the Internet, any web addresses or links contained in this book may have changed since publication and may no longer be valid. The views expressed in this work are solely those of the author and do not necessarily reflect the views of the publisher, and the publisher hereby disclaims any responsibility for them.

NO!

Contents

Introduction vii
   It all begins with a loving "Yes!" viii
   An honest "No!" is a loving answer xi
   Write your own job description xv

Saying "No!" to children 1
   "No!" and our personal values 5
   From birth 7
   From the ages one to five 12
   Language 21
   Needs and wants 32
   "What do you want?" 42

When should we say "No!"? 49
   The reflective "No!" 50
   The spontaneous "No!" 54

When "No!" is non-negotiable 56
Without a "No!" there is no "Yes!" 60
The autonomous child 62
Saying "No!" to tweens and teenagers 65

The personal "No!" 73
The male and the female "No!" 81
Saying "No!" to your partner 84

Introduction

"Can I stay up late tonight?"
"Well, you are still young . . . and you are very tired."

"Why can't I have a tattoo?"
"But you know they look really cheap."

"I want an ice cream!"
"It is not good for you. You might get a sore tummy."

"Darling, how about we go to bed early and relax as soon as the kids are asleep?"
"Do you honestly feel things are relaxed at the moment?"

"I don't want to go to school."
"Ah, come on! You love school."

"Darling, I think we should visit your parents this Easter."
"But last week you said we never have enough time for each other."

"Can I have some money for the party on Saturday?"
"What happened to your pocket money? You got some the day before yesterday."

These are common and very reasonable questions. But what is going to happen next? The answers were not exactly clear . . .

It all begins with a loving "Yes!"

A loving relationship always begins with a "Yes!"

Simply deciding to spend time with someone is in itself a way of saying "Yes!" to that person. Through conversation we verbally confirm our love in a number of direct and more subtle ways. We say "Yes!" when we decide to live together and perhaps marry. So we confirm that our love is ready to be put into practice and carried out on a daily basis.

By formalizing our feelings through one little word we are ready to begin our shared journeys. The "Yes!" marks the reality that fulfillment of a dream is within reach. It also comes with all the commitments and responsibilities that are inevitably part of a shared life.

Every newborn or adopted child has the right to experience this important feeling of acceptance. They should be able to see the loving "Yes!" when they look into their parents' eyes and sense it in their expressions. This is "Yes!" to a shared starting point of a long journey together.

There are moments in our lives when that little word is not only the most valued treasure but also the biggest gift of all. It is the most telling symbol of someone's trust, honesty and willingness to create a space where loneliness no longer exists. It can be an overwhelming yet humbling privilege to receive a first "Yes!" Be it as a pubescent kiss, the exciting "Yes!" at a wedding and of course the gaze into a little baby's trusting eyes. We are so humbled by this loving feeling that we excitedly promise ourselves to do everything in our power to be deserving of this "Yes!"

Yet, this commitment that came with the strongest dedication and best intentions, tends to fade in the midst of our daily routines. Gradually, the "Yes!" ceases to be a gift so freely given. It slowly becomes something that is expected, demanded or a duty. The other person is aware of this—in fact, both sides of the "Yes!" are aware of it. Things are taken for granted and much is expected. The teacher expects students' respect, the in-laws expect to be visited and so on. The pleasure we experience from receiving as well as giving decreases and the love and trust with which it was initially meant disappears just as quickly. In a relationship this is most dramatically felt during the so-called, *seven-year itch*. When it comes to the relationship with our children it has most likely happened by the point they have learned to speak and their autonomy brings some kind of discord in the parent's hopes and expectations.

Important changes occur when parents stop saying "Yes!" with their hearts and say "No!" through their behavior. Or when we just say "Yeah, yeah . . ." which really means "No!"

Then dishonesty enters the relationship and everyone feels trapped. However, the love that exists between parents and children does not die so easily.

An honest "No!" is a loving answer

At some stage, children will start to say "No!" yet parents often forget to see this as a gift. Children do not use this little word to whine about something. From time to time parents might use "No!" as a whine—but not children. Their "No!" is used with all the good intentions, innocence and honesty of a child. Parents unfortunately, often take this "No!" personally because it is difficult to hear that children actually say "No!" to themselves. When young children say "No!" they have no intention of crossing their parents. They use "No!" to define themselves and their personal boundaries. They also use "No!" in order for the parents to learn who the child really is—their child that loves them so completely and unconditionally. Children have no carefully conceived motives behind saying "No!" but it pays to think of the "No!" as including intentions of unconditional love.

Much has been said and written about how important it is for children to have boundaries and that adults are able to control children's behavior. These issues play a dominant part in the field of child-psychology. So much in fact, that you are forgiven for thinking that this is what parenting and child development is all about. This thinking has a widespread and very dedicated following. Accusations of irresponsibility and laziness quickly become the labels that stick to those parents who do not set strict boundaries. This is strongly supported by another primitive trend in children's upbringing and pedagogy. Namely, the increasing popularity of super-nannies, boot-camps and pop-psychology which claims to be able to convert any troublesome family into a calm, clean and structured unit in just a few days. The people behind these approaches try to convince us that theirs is the best way to live.

It is noticeable and indeed worrying that the need for setting boundaries is growing at the very same time when children's physical and emotional spaces are decreasing. Most people think that children have become more liberated in their interactions with adults. They also think children have become super-consumers, but they tend to forget the fact that it is no longer possible for children to play, live and grow or indeed do anything without adult supervision. Just a generation ago children had plenty of space and time without adults. That is exactly how they developed what we today call "social competence". This is something neither parents, schools, kindergartens or any other institution can teach children. No matter how hard adults try. Today's child has to be "well-functioning"—a label that is glued to children making it impossible for them to move freely.

For exactly that reason, this book is not designed to support those parents who see a need to set fixed limits and strict boundaries for their children. We do not want to support anyone's desire to control or gain power over others — children or adults.

On the contrary, this book is all about the quality of our relationships and how important it is that we are able to say "No!" to others, as this is the only way we are able to say "Yes!" to ourselves.

We need to learn to define our own personal boundaries —and as part of that process define ourselves. This is as important for our own lives as it is for the relationships and communities we are part of. We can do this with a very clear conscience for the simple reason that we will provide a good role model for our children.

It is first and foremost through loving relationships with others that we are able to learn about ourselves on a deeper and a more profound level. It is when we love others that we voluntarily open ourselves up and become vulnerable. It is, in fact, through loving relationships that we happily and willingly cross our usual boundaries in exchange for the joy of sharing and being together. We will naturally discover new aspects of our own personality as we and indeed our relationships mature. Some boundaries completely disappear whilst others appear or resurface more distinctly. Old wounds heal and inevitably new ones are opened. Within the family we are, figuratively speaking, bruised, wounded, scratched and hurt. Whilst this is uncomfortable, it is also something we learn from. We do grow because we learn about ourselves and others. We learn to care for the wounded, to respect others as well as set our own personal boundaries so we develop as individuals with unique personalities. As we feel better about ourselves we also develop the ability to engage ourselves more deeply with each other—most importantly, and as a consequence, we also learn to step back and say "No!" to what we do not want in our lives. Ultimately, this growth allows us to become more relaxed as well as easier and more enriching to spend time with.

Write your own job description

This book is written with the utmost respect for you as a parent. For the first time in the history of mankind you will have to write your job description from the inside out. Your role as a parent has to be based on your own thoughts, feelings and values because there are no cultural or professional guidelines you can hang onto or simply copy. As if this is not challenging enough, you are also required to develop and maintain a relationship with your partner that is based on equality and respect. You are also expected to meet your obligations to the wider community. For that to be possible it becomes increasingly important to be able to say "No!" to a whole range of requests and demands.

It really is difficult saying "No!" because it has to come from the inside and it has to be personal. And of course it has to make an impact, otherwise you will keep repeating the old: *"How many times do I have to tell you!"* and *"Why don't you understand . . . ? I have already told you at least a hundred times!"* Saying this a number of times and you are certain to lose your dignity and respect.

Not until we are able to say "No!" to each other are we able to say "Yes!" to ourselves. Not surprisingly, the opposite applies too. We can say "Yes!" with sincerity and honesty only when we are also willing and able to say "No!"—whenever that is what we really feel.

Saying "No!" to children

From our own experiences we know that saying "Yes!" to our children is preferable—all the time. We want to do everything for them even to the point of sacrificing our own lives for theirs. It makes sense because "Yes!", as we know, is a symbol of love and thus a way of confirming that everything between us is the way it ought to be. Essentially, there is nothing wrong with saying "Yes!" all the time—if it is said genuinely, lovingly and completely without expectations or hidden agendas. However, we must acknowledge that this is not always possible.

When we study the literature about raising children it is clearly evident that it has always been challenging for parents to say "No!" to their children. During some periods parents have said "No!" far too often, whilst at other times not often enough. The generation of the mid 1900s by and large chose the strategy of saying "No!"—just in case. It mostly came with a stern look and an angry voice which simply meant that they really wanted to say "Yes!" instead. *"No means no! There should be no reason to say this more than once!"* or *"You don't ask! Wait until you are offered!"* This was how parents ensured their children's obedience.

In the early 1990s things changed and parents mostly chose a different strategy. They simply said "Yes!"—again, just in case. This time, their hesitations, pauses, resigning shoulders and their contradicting tone of voice told us that they really wanted to say "No!".

There are around 50 years between these two approaches. And this is evident in the ways their discomfort was handled. Moreover, the approaches are rooted in two completely different societies. The first mentioned generation from the mid 1900s grew up in a society when there was a real material shortage. It was also a time when parents knew how to bring up children simply because they carried on a tradition. This meant that they knew when "Yes!" or "No!" was most appropriate. Very often they had no choice but to say "No!", as they could not afford to give their children what they wanted. Parents who were more affluent and could afford it were looked upon as spoiling their children—of course this was often mixed with some degree of envy.

Comparatively, today's parents are affluent and we live in a consumer society. Through our affluence we have to a large extent defined our personalities through consumption. We have become consumers and so have our children. Parents carry home huge shopping bags with their eyes shining as bright as the stars—thanks to the endorphins released in the brain from satisfying shopping needs. Gone are those norms, rules and values that were so much part of the previous generation and their real financial hardship.

Most families are able to find ways of getting by in this consumer society. It does not make a noticeable dent in their budgets should the children want one, two or five ice creams on a hot summer's day. Or if an outfit costs an extra 10% compared to a cheaper version. Parents are most likely able to find a way to buy things anyway purely out of consideration for the children's status amongst their peers—or their own status amongst other parents. There is nothing new in the fact that children play an important role in promoting their parents' excellence, wealth and status (or compensating for lack of the same!)

Wealth, no doubt, is one of the reasons why parents simply do not need to say "No!" to their children. But there are other underlying reasons. Some parents are reluctant to confront their children, some are lazy, some want to turn the atmosphere of the family into total bliss and harmony, and some parents do not have enough control over their own lives to say "No!", while others simply get the concept of being "child-friendly" completely wrong.

Before we take a look at some of these families let us take a closer look at why it is so important to be able to say "No!" to our children. As with most things that happen within the family it is not so important *what* we do or say. *How we* say it and *why* we do so has a much greater impact. There is absolutely no reason to believe that everything will be fine if we just say "No!" a specified amount of times. On the other hand, there is plenty of evidence to show that if we say "Yes!" in a half-hearted, guarded, dishonest or defensive way it will be destructive for a healthy relationship between ourselves and our children.

"No!" and our personal values

Many of us find it difficult to grasp how a "No!" can be a loving answer. Yet, it is crucially important for a good relationship between two people. Were we to analyze our own lives we would find that many of our conflicts came about because people did not say "No!" even though this was in fact what they really meant. This happens when we do not express ourselves clearly or are unable to define what it is we really want. Perhaps a "No!" is not appropriate in certain families and cultures or maybe some family members do not like it's negative connotations. We must remember that "No!" rarely is rejection. When it feels like that, it is because we have failed to look after our own personal boundaries and needs. When things go wrong we will, more often than not, try to resolve our own discomfort by blaming others. The art of saying "No!" is all about taking responsibility for ourselves—for our own sakes and certainly for the sake of our relationships with others.

There are plenty of very plausible reasons why we should shy away from saying "No!".

We do not like to upset others; instead we end up hurting them.
We try to avoid confrontation right here and now; instead we end up with plenty of confrontations later.
We really want others to like us; instead we end up loathing each other and perhaps ourselves.
We strive to be popular; instead we end up being used as doormats.
We hope to be kind and sympathetic; instead we end up coming across as dismissive and stand-offish.
We strive to be open and generous; instead we end up grumpy and scrupulous.

Behind all these motives lies our fundamental need to know that we have value. We need to feel valued by those we love. This need does not manifest itself more acutely than in the relationships with our children. We wish to give children everything we possibly can—and most importantly—a better life than we had ourselves. A combination of this fundamental need to feel valued and our human desire to improve things for the next generation is without doubt a crucial reason why it is so difficult to find a healthy balance between "Yes!" and "No!".

"No!" requires careful consideration, deep engagement, bold courage and absolute honesty. Precisely because of this, it is the most difficult answer. It is also the most loving answer.

From birth

Young babies do not experience this dilemma and find it easy to express themselves. They "say" it to their parents long before they learn to speak. When they are being breast-fed and have had enough they simply turn their heads, fall asleep or spit the milk out. They might protest when they are handed over to strangers and cry when we want them to go to sleep but they are not yet ready for sleep. It is also during this stage when parents cross their own boundaries and downgrade their personal needs out of consideration for the baby.

As is evident, there is an explicit difference between the child's natural ability to say "No!" and the parents' duty to say "Yes!" This creates the first real conflict between them. It often requires a substantial amount of self-control by the parents.

Nevertheless, even the smallest children have a natural desire to co-operate. They will adjust whenever they are able to and really do prefer saying "Yes!" to their parents—and to everything around them. All they require is to feel safe and comfortable when they are with their parents. It is this innate need for safety that so many parents aim to provide which makes them say "Yes!" to the children—give them every little thing they seem to want and need.

In times gone by, parents tried to satisfy these needs by setting strict limits, fixed boundaries and sticking to these regardless of the child's protests (the famous pediatrician, Dr. Benjamin Spock tried to comfort mothers by telling them that crying was healthy for the development of their lungs).

These days parents with children younger than 18 months will mostly need to respond to their children's needs with a "Yes!" which means they say "No!" to their own needs. When the child wakes up crying, parents give up their own need for sleep. When the child is ill, parents rearrange their own plans. When the baby needs changing, parents stop what they are doing. This however, should not mean that parents must sacrifice themselves completely and say "No!" to their own values, feelings and goals. If this were to happen they would not be able to assume the leadership role that is fundamental for children to feel safe.

When nursing a three month old infant in the middle of the night it is perfectly alright to wish and hope for them to fall asleep straight away. There is no reason to feel guilty about that feeling. Parents need to maintain their own personal needs at the same time as they meet the baby's needs. If they do not they might loose themselves and let the baby take over. The inner voice must say: "It is my decision to nurse you until you calm down. You don't make me do this—I want to do it." When that happens the baby senses leadership and confidence, and will co-operate as a result. Should parents not pick this up during the first couple of months, they will become "victims" which does not do anyone any good.

We all know that leadership is not about bossing others around and getting things the way we want them. It is all about representing some ideals and goals. When this is done with enough integrity others will want to co-operate.

At FamilyLab we often speak with couples who bring their babies along to the counseling sessions. The baby might be sound asleep and the conversation runs smoothly until suddenly the baby makes a few noises. Both parents stop and turn around. Often they pick up the baby, resulting in a long break because they check on the baby, try to rock it back to sleep, or whatever. Other couples will return to the conversation without picking up the baby and demonstrate that this is important for them right now. Nine out of ten times the baby will go straight back to sleep. It is exactly this ability to stand by their own needs, without forgetting the baby, which characterizes good leadership and makes the children feel safe. It also ensures that the relationship is based on equality.

The parents in the first example forget their own needs and worry on behalf of their children. They might not be sure what is required of them in the situation. This worry or insecurity is very quickly transferred to the child who will in turn become unsettled and, not surprisingly, difficult to calm down.

Small children have a phenomenally well-developed ability to do what researchers have named: "in-tuning"—the baby's ability to sense or "tune in to" their parents' feelings and moods. This remarkable ability is at work day and night and they are able to sense this over long distances. It is what makes it possible for a baby to co-operate with their parents, but when the parents are highly insecure, anxious or frustrated the baby cannot work out who and what they are dealing with. They simply receive too many different and conflicting messages from their parents. This is, in fact, the reason why parents often find it difficult to get their children to go to sleep around the ages of 18 to 36 months. It is also what sometimes makes it challenging for parents to hand their babies over to strangers.

From the ages one to five

From around 18 months most children can move around independently. They understand what adults say and are developing their own active language. Their parents have had the opportunity to learn more about who their children are. Their personality starts to show and any parent will have learned more about their own personality and about themselves as parents. At this stage they will have the opportunity to step into character that in turn gives the child the opportunity to find out about their parents as people who are much more than service providers. If parents do not show their true colors, the child will continue to expect the high service level to which they have become accustomed. This is, after all, the kind of love the baby has experiences all it's life—be it only 18 months long.

Service however, is not the same as love. When the two are mistaken the child easily gets locked in the past wanting more and more service. The parents will inevitably become frustrated as they are overwhelmed with the demands and so they will fail themselves and each other. If the parents then resort to hiring nannies and baby-sitters, the children will start living artificial lives. They will experience adults who are there for them and they will not realize that people also have their own feelings, emotions, needs and boundaries. These children will often become unhappy and lonely—and might end up using and abusing others.

This scenario seems to become more and more widespread as children from the age of six months spend an increasing amount of time in childcare. Generally speaking, staff in childcare centers are highly professional. Nevertheless, they are with the children for the sake of the children and are as such in the role of service providers. In other words, in these contexts children are not interacting with ordinary adults who have their own lives, faults and failures. They interact with people who essentially "work" for them.

In many childcare centers and similar institutions the adults' personal boundaries and needs disappear only to make room for set standards and regulations. Most of the pedagogical staff is excellent, highly professional and get on really well with the children. Because of this many parents see them as role models. Ultimately and unfortunately, some of the important differences between institution and family disappear. So does the difference between professional adult and parent, and pedagogy and up-bringing. As a result, many children do not experience proper and equal relationships. When parents copy pedagogues and teachers in an attempt to spend quality time with their children one thing is certain: the children will become increasingly frustrated as their need for personal and equally valued relationships are not met. To make things worse, their need for entertainment and externally generated stimulation grows.

The only way to counter this trend is for parents to be as genuine and authentic as humanly possible. This will create space for parents to be adults and provide children with the opportunity to develop their social skills as well as learn to accept other people's boundaries and needs.

Small children will, by nature, constantly cross their parents' boundaries. This is not out of a lack of respect. It is simply because they are so engaged with their own needs and desires. They are also very attentive to the answers they are given. They soak these up like little sponges—along with any other signals parents send. Children's behavior serves two purposes: to satisfy their needs and to get to know their parents. They need to work out what their parents like and do not like, what they want and do not want, and what they will accept and what they will not. During the next three to four years they will slowly but surely search for the answers until they have integrated their parents' ideas of what is right and wrong, good and bad, etc. This is how children copy our moral concepts.

This process will first and foremost require clarity from our side—and repetition. We must be patient and repeat until things are firmly entrenched in their consciousness. Some things take just a few weeks whilst others take years and years. The more the child is told off and criticized—the longer it takes. The more insecure and critical the environment—the longer it takes to learn new ways of interacting—if it happens at all.

Children operate as researchers not as students. They have to experiment to be able to reach their own conclusions. All they really need from their parents is trust and gentle guidance. A very unfortunate alternative to this is physical and psychological violence. This only leads to a lack of respect for the parents, their boundaries and needs. They learn to doubt themselves and to fear authority and punishment.

When a two-year-old pulls at your glasses for the third time you could say: *"Stop, I don't want that."* (in a gentle but firm and confident voice) and then take the glasses. Or say: "I can see that you find my glasses interesting to play with but I don't want it." Then take the glasses.

When a four-year-old interrupts your conversation over dinner you could say: *"I want to finish the conversation with Jane first then I want to speak with you."*

These are very clear, personal and constructive messages. They are much easier for children to deal with than these examples of traditional up-bringing: *"No, no darling . . . Glasses are not for playing with. They cost a lot of money."* or "We don't interrupt when others are speaking. You'll have to wait."

Alternatively, the dad says: *"Your dad doesn't want you to play with his glasses."* or: *"Your father just wants to speak with your mother first."* When parents speak about themselves in third person there is very little chance that they will be heard—let alone have their boundaries and needs respected. Imagine if an adult said to you: *"Liz doesn't want to speak with you right now."* or *"John is not able to look after the children tomorrow."* We would not appreciate that.

Let us take a quick look at the incorrectly labeled "terrible twos". When children go through that phase many parents become defensive and say "No!" more often than they would really like to.

During that phase children become less dependent and more independent. This is, all things considered, very beneficial to the parents as they will gain more freedom, more personal time and more time for each other. Their children can move around more freely, communicate more confidently and explore their world more independently. Everything needs to be explored, tested and tried. They demand to do things on their own—and do them their own way—even the things they are not able to do yet.

During this phase children have two important needs: they need their parents' feedback and plenty of support and encouragement. The feedback must reflect the parents' values and boundaries which means it will be necessary to say "No!" on countless occasions. The more personal and confident the adults are able to express themselves, the sooner their little explorers will reach their conclusions. *"No, I don't want to buy sweets today!"*, *"I don't want you to pull the pots and pans out of the cupboard today!"*, *"No, you cannot stay up late tonight. I have had a really difficult day today and I need some quiet time now."* or *"I would love to hear about all the wonderful things that happened at kindergarten today but you will have to wait. First, I want to say "Hi!" to dad and chat with him."*

The more critical, blaming or defensive the parents' feedback is, the harder children will fight for answers they find acceptable and can live with. *"Listen darling, I have told you before that you can't have sweets every day. You cannot come shopping when you behave like that!"*, *"Who do you think is going to clean up all this stuff afterwards?"*, *"If you don't go to bed on time you won't have enough energy to play at kindergarten tomorrow. We have spoken about that a* number of times before." or *"Darling, of course your mother would love to hear about your day in kindergarten, but don't you think it could wait until she has a bit more time?"*

The other part of their development is their desire for independence and autonomy. This will need plenty of support and encouragement. You need to be positive and say "Yes!" to that. Whenever they want to do things by themselves it is a good idea to say: *"Try and see if you can work it out now. If you need help, just let me know."* There is no doubt about the fact that you are able to save a lot of time if you do it for them, but the sooner they learn to do it by themselves the sooner you do not have to do it at all.

The most beneficial way of looking at a two-year-old is to see this phase as a gift. In 18 months time this gift will give you more time and more freedom. If you are able to say "Yes!" to that, it will be much easier to say "No!" which you will have to do on many occasions.

This period in a child's development is to some extent similar to puberty. It is their first opportunity to get a look into who they are and establish more active relationships with their parents.

Caring for children under two years of age is a source of great satisfaction for parents. It also provides a very real experience of being valued and a sense of purpose. However, it is just as important that the young children being cared for feel that they are being valued. This requires parents to find other ways of satisfying their need to feel valued.

We cannot deny the fact that having children is in many ways a self-centered project. Deep down, it is about our desire to be able to give, to love and to care for others. All this is perfectly fine. It simply requires that we are able to relate to our children with a loving balance between our personal self-centered desires and openness towards their personality and needs. The things that make parents feel useful are not necessarily the things that also make our children feel valued. This does not happen until we receive, acknowledge and appreciate all that they give us. And this is exactly what develops and stimulates our self-esteem. The world is already full of parents who are sufficiently self-centered to think that their children are ungrateful.

Language

We communicate with each other by means of words, tone of voice and body language. Preferably, these are in harmony during communication. Adults and children are very adept detecting inconsistencies between these features, and this leads to misunderstanding and frustration. Effective communication takes place when "words and music are linked".

Adults tend to talk to infants using a "light" tone of voice, and body language that is very friendly. The words do not seem to matter much to newborns. Around the age of six months it starts to become more important that the language (words and sentences) and music (tone of voice) develop and become more nuanced. It is not only important that the child feels welcome, loved and safe, the time has also come for the them to learn about our feelings, emotions and intentions—and they are also learning language. Even by 6 months of age, children have already experienced a a variety of emotions and language yet, they have very little understanding of why, how and what it all means.

Since the 1970s it has been seen as both right and necessary to adjust adult language to a level that children can understand. Parents and early childhood teachers go to great lengths to use short sentences and simple words. This friendliness and consideration for the child's linguistic competencies is without doubt beneficial to teaching them fine motor skills as well as building their intellectual capacity. However, this approach is not such a good idea when the aim is to develop intimate, safe and respectful relationships.

Many parents will from time to time use an artificial language. One option is the appealing "teacher-like" version which focuses being positive: *"No, no my little friend . . . You do know that dad doesn't really want you to touch his computer when it is on. One day when you get your own then dad will show you how to use it."* The other option is the stern and serious version: *"I don't know how many times I need to say this . . . You know you are not allowed to touch dad's computer!"*

In both examples they speak to the children in a way they imagine "real" parents speak. As a result their personality disappears. Consequently, they will experience many conflicts with the children and they both become confused and driven to despair. This happens because the parents set the tone in the family and interactions become a role-play where parents as well as children play childish games. The family will never become a family of adults and children being their true selves. Rather, the family becomes a concept which everyone tries desperately to live up to.

When we use this kind of "child friendly" language we weaken the message and we fall short of making the right impression. Our emotions are no longer connected to the words we use. This makes it difficult for us to communicate who we are as people. This communication ignores important messages about our boundaries, desires, needs and what is important to us.

Almost daily we meet parents who are unhappy and frustrated because their children do not listen to what they say, do not co-operate or do not understand the messages parents try to communicate. Parents say: *"If only you knew how many times we have told him . . . !"* When they describe their children's behavior it does indeed sound like they are reluctant, not co-operating and completely indifferent to what their parents say. With very few exceptions, their behavior will change as soon as the parents find ways to connect their emotions to the words they say. This actually applies not only to the small daily conflicts but also to the bigger and more difficult ones—especially those that are emotionally dramatic such as moving house, separation, death and illness.

The *way* you say it makes all the difference. Here are some common examples—

Say: *"I want you to clean up now!"* (in a clearly irritated tone of voice.)
Do not say: *"Your mother gets really frustrated when you don't clean up after yourself."* (in a blaming, appealing or "teacher-like" tone of voice.)

Say: *"I want you to tidy your room. Would you do that please?"*
Do not say: *"Why does your room always look like a rubbish tip?"*

Say: *"I am tired and need to rest for a while. I would like you to be quiet for 30 minutes."*

Do not say: *"Couldn't you stop making such noise—just for once!"*

It is not a question of speaking *nicely* but about sending a personal message. We are all required to speak nicely when we are at work and amongst strangers. This is our "social language" which is suitable when we wish to maintain a professional or personal distance and if we try to avoid having an emotional influence on others. "Social language" however, is not suitable when we wish to establish personal relationships. This is noticeable in the conflicts with our children and partners. Speaking nicely does not suffice during conflicts and arguments, so we resort to using foul and perhaps offensive language simply because we find it difficult to express ourselves personally.

This difference is important. When we are able to express ourselves personally it is impossible to offend or hurt others. Instead, we are likely to define and use labels. For example, stating *"You are a pain!"* instead of *"I felt hurt by that."* We do this because we forget to show a genuine interest in the other person. Nobody, neither children nor adults, like to be defined or labeled by others. A positive and flattering label only comes a poor second ranked just below the labels that are critical and put people down.

When we express ourselves on a personal level we make an important impression on others. They might be surprised, saddened, frustrated or angry, but we will never push their boundaries or offend their personal integrity. There is nothing wrong with having an emotional impact. That is after all, the whole idea—but we should not offend them.

Within our family the social language of society does not suffice. The problem is that conversations can turn ugly because parents are not able to (or forget to) express their needs, wishes and boundaries in a clear and personal language. Here are some examples—

"I want you to clean the kitchen table every time you make a sandwich!" Do not say: *"Don't you think I've got better things to do than clean up after you..!?"* Do not say: *"Do you really think I am asking too much of you? I just don't want to be your personal servant. You will have to help out!"*

"Listen, when it comes to your sports bag I want to do things differently. From now on, it will be your responsibility to empty your bag and put the gear in the wash!" Do not say: *"Again and again, I have to empty your sports bag. How many times have I told you that it isn't my responsibility. What will your teacher be thinking about me when you always turn up without your sports gear?"* Do not say: *"Your sports gear is on the table young man! What would you do if I didn't think for you all the time?"* Do not say: *"Why can't you just do some simple things for yourself? We are not exactly asking too much of you so at least you could look after your own sports gear!"*

Instead of getting angry, parents might try to be teacher-like, nice or attempt to be popular. By doing so they end up offending their own personal integrity. They often say: *"We tried 'the nice way' first but it didn't work."* But they are also saying that their first attempt was an act and not a real genuine attempt. They do not notice this because they are too preoccupied doing the "right" thing. Yet, the children are hurt, sad and angry and will sooner or later start using foul language. The parents will certainly notice that!

When we do not express ourselves in a personal manner we speak 'with forked tongues'. The words say one thing but the tone of voice conveys something different. Younger children get confused and do not know which message they need to take seriously. More often than not, they will relate to what we do and not to what we say. For example:

"Don't you know how disappointed your mother gets when you don't stick to the agreements we make. I am really trying to ask you as nicely as possible but I don't know what to do anymore." Said by a mother who was furious because her son did not put his toys away even though he had promised to do so. She says this as she throws the toys into the toy box. What message is the boy getting here?

Older children and teenagers will often stop listening altogether. They do this simply because what is said is not worth listening to. The adults wrap up their personal messages and children do not want to unwrap them. They might reply to the actual wording and ignore the rest—or the other way around. When young people put their silence into words they say: *"Why don't you just say what it is you* want?" or *"Just tell me what it is you are thinking. I am sick and tired of guessing!"*

In western societies we are not usually held responsible for the tone of voice or the "music" of what we say. What counts are the words. Within the family on the other hand we are held accountable for the whole message—even when it is contradictory or vague. Most of the time we try to relate to the personal messages communicated by those we are close to. The further these messages are hidden behind critical, appealing or bland statements the less we receive of what we really need, namely closeness, acknowledgement and empathy.

Many parents will find it unnecessarily brash to say: *"I want . . ."* and *"No!"* It is not seen as polite or politically correct to focus on yourself in that manner. Softer and more subtle statements are preferred. It is, in fact, a very good idea and absolutely possible to be more direct. When parents use direct language over a longer period of time their leadership and personal boundaries will have manifested themselves in such a manner that the children know exactly what their parents stand for. To begin with it is a good idea to use a more nuanced and even indirect language such as:

> *"I don't think you should do that!", "I don't think that is a good idea!"* or *"I think that is quite enough!"*

Many parents who become frustrated because they lack clout and authority in relation to their children will also experience similar frustration in relation to other adults. This might be with their partner, parents-in-law, employer, colleagues or others. They experience a lack of respect and feel used, hurt or ignored. These are similar feelings to those experienced as a parent — children have a unique ability to pressure our most tender spots. Hopefully, this knowledge will eventually help us become better parents and adults.

Of course, frustration and feelings of inadequacy do not feature in all relationships between parents and children. Many parents let go of their personal authority because they think that raising children ought to be some kind of democratic paradise without any signs of disagreement. In some ways it sounds appealing and idyllic but unfortunately it always ends in disharmony. This is so because the principles of raising children are not political, neither should they be about power. Life within the family is not about who wins. It is about ensuring that everyone gets as much as possible of what they need, and as little as possible of what might hurt them. A family trying to live in a democratic paradise will essentially have to prioritize the community's harmony higher than the individual's boundaries and needs.

The better you are able to connect what you say with who you are, the more your self-esteem will grow and you will gain respect and understanding from others. You will also experience your children's increased desire and willingness to co-operate. You will have less conflicts and less frustration. A person who is not able to set their own personal boundaries is like a fruit orchard without a fence—anyone can walk in and help themselves at the expense of the owner. It is also likely that those who have abused your boundaries will become confused and frustrated.

It is not difficult to understand that there is a temptation to use "child-friendly" language and a sweet tone of voice. It is indeed a logical counter action to the traditional and authoritarian language that was offending, hurting, humiliating or violent.

The language of love is neither positive nor negative—it is personal.

Needs and wants

Obviously, the most important duty of any parent is to fulfill their children's fundamental needs for belonging, closeness, safety, food, care, clothes, warmth and rest. In addition to that, you might have the option of also giving them some of what they want.

They do not have an imminent knowledge of the difference between that they need and the things they want. The poverty of previous generations and their authoritarian ways of ruling the family resulted in children's longing for freedom—a freedom to do and have exactly what they wanted. These children have now become parents and the desire for freedom is still deeply ingrained in us and is, in fact, one of the reasons why we for many years have had a tendency to provide this freedom and let the family budget be ruled by our children's wants.

We can spoil children by giving them too much of the things they want. Spoilt children will not take a "*No!*" for an answer. They always expect to get what they want which makes them demanding and annoying. Children only develop this way because they get too much of the wrong things—and most importantly—for the wrong reasons.

In an affluent society it is challenging not to give children what they want. It requires integrity and strong morals. They constantly ask for whatever it is they want at any particular moment. It is up to the parents to consider this fundamental question: "*Am I genuinely able to give my child what they want and feel good about it—and not expect anything in return?*"

If the answer is "*Yes!*" a series of moral, political and religious questions arise. Parents need to be able to provide these answers with their integrity intact.

Let us look at an example: Do your children have more toys than they *need*? Reality is that children do not need toys. All they really need is something to play with. Toys are simply something they want because they think it will give them pleasure to own these or because they have seen them at a friend's place, in a shop or advertised. This does not mean that all toys are essentially bad—it only means that the parents will have to make some important decisions.

Most of today's parents grew up in an affluent society. Some might feel very comfortable as consumers and happy to give their children what they ask for. If that is the case, there is no reason to fear that this causes any harm to the child or damages the relationship between the parent and the child.

The parents might want to take political, moral and ethical issues into consideration. Some struggle with the macro-economic issue of wealth distribution between developed and developing countries. Perhaps they consider the option of letting older children share part of the cost of what they want. This might enable them to learn about the value of money and they will possibly start to think differently about quality, longevity, the environment and production methods. These considerations might limit consumption. Neither will this harm children or the relationships with their parents.

Similarly, children and young people want plenty of other things too. They need food and want a pizza or a burger but nutrition is their parents' responsibility. It is absolutely possible to live a happy childhood without ever eating at a fast food restaurant or having take-away. During the first 10 years of a child's life their parents can practice this according to their own values. Let's consider this conversation—

- "Can we have take-away tonight?"
- "No, I don't want that!"
- "But . . . Why not?"
- "Because I don't want to spend my money on bad quality food."
- "But . . . Paul, Laura and Michael's parents let them have it. Why can't we?"
- "Their parents apparently think differently to me."
- "Why can't you think like they do?"
- "I guess, I could. But I don't want to."

— "You are a strange!"
— "I can understand that you feel like that but that is the kind of mother you have."
— "I just think it is unfair. When my friend's parents let them have it."
— "I really do understand that you want take-away but it will have to wait until you can decide these things. I don't want it."
— "I'll get angry with you . . . Really angry!"
— "That's all right with me if you are really angry."
— "I am!"
— "All right. I hope you get over it."

The conflict is over and done with, and both of them can walk away with their dignity and integrity intact.

Children and young people need clothes. Very often they want the brand that advertising people are trying to make popular. Here is an example conversation—

— "Considering I need new jeans couldn't we buy X-jeans? They are on sale and everyone else wears them. Can I have a pair as well?"

— "What do they cost?"

— "They cost $100 but next week they are 10% off. It really is cheap and it is going to take a long time before they are on sale again. Lots of my friends have already got them."

— "Even though they only cost $100 they are still too expensive. Quite frankly, we can't afford to buy such expensive clothes in our family."

— "You always say that! How come the others can afford it. Are we really that poor?"

— "No, we are not poor, but we just don't have that kind of money and we can't buy whatever we would like to—even though it could be nice to be able to."

— "And what if the others tease and bully me because I am the only one who is not allowed to get a pair? How much fun do you think that is going to be?"

— "I can understand that you would like to follow the latest fashion. I truly hope that you will not accept being bullied because it simply isn't possible to buy those jeans. I am happy to go shopping with you to look for a pair that is fashionable and cheaper. Or you might want to call Julia and explain the situation to her, perhaps she can help you find a pair. She is your best friend and is often able to come up with good ideas."

— "What if I ask grandma? Maybe she will buy them for me."

— "You are welcome to call her. Remember, I have nothing against the jeans you want and I would really like to be able to fulfill all your wishes but I can't do that all the time."

— "Cool! Can I tell grandma that you suggested it."

— "No, you can't do that. It was your idea and it is your responsibility."

Another example of how the parent says "No!"—this time to two wishes—without the parent nor the child getting hurt or the relationship between them suffering.

The first example illustrated a conflict between the parent's values and the child's wish. The second was a conflict between a desire and the family economy. Both examples also deal with another issue which plays an important part of everyone's consciousness: the need to belong—and thereby the fear of being excluded. This makes a lot of

No!

people want to conform whilst others prefer to seek their individuality.

To what extent do we need to take into consideration the child's fear of being excluded from the friendship group? This depends on a number of things:

If the child says: *"But everyone else has one!"* it is likely to be part of the sales pitch, and then you will know that it does not matter so much. However, if the child also becomes stifled with sobs, becomes shifty-eyed and you can see fear in their eyes, then there might be an underlying problem. It will be important to speak about that at another time. When children have most of their attention focused on other people's expectations and find if difficult to feel comfortable and think independently then they need their parents help. They need a healthier balance between individuality and conformity. This might be an opportunity for you to assess how you view them so you do not expect something of the child that you yourself are not prepared or able to live up to. In case there is pressure from others in the group then you might be able to speak with the whole group. You will be able to learn something about the situation as well as help the children reflect on what it is they are doing to themselves and each other. Just make sure not to lecture to them. Be direct and friendly. For example—

— "Listen girls, Sarah and I have spoken about what kind of jeans we should buy and she would obviously prefer a pair of X-jeans. The problem is, we cannot afford to buy such expensive jeans and she is worried that she might be teased and bullied by the rest of you. Is that a risk?"
— "Not by us, really. But maybe some of the others might comment and tease those who are not up with the latest . . ?"
— "Do you accept that?"
— "Well . . . we might have to. Of course, it depends on how we feel. It can be difficult if we are not feeling well."
— "I understand that. I hope you will be able to help each other instead of trying to be smart about it! Thanks for your help."

When adults level with teenagers as in this example it makes an important impression. Much better than when the adults lecture or start moralizing. We should never make a big deal out of fighting for our children's causes in front of their friends. This is humiliating and increases the risk of them being bullied.

Parents have a variety of ideological attitudes which will influence their choice of "Yes!" or "No!" In general, two rules of thumb apply:

1. When parents are against something children want it is advisable to keep ideological influences under wraps. Talk about it some other time when neither is busy pursuing their agendas.

2. Until the time when young people reach puberty parents are able to use their ideological power to make decisions. Thereafter, their ideology and attitude ought to be put on the same footing as the child's. They have listened to their parents' opinions all of their lives. Time has come for them to express their own.

"What do you want?"

This question is part of the heritage which today's parents have to deal with. During the 1970s and 1980s people celebrated their newfound freedom to follow their desires and did what they wanted. This was in many ways an antidote to the duties they were brought up with. It was simply an effort to create space for the individual within the confines of the community—a well-founded political rebellion. When people asked each other: *"What do you want?"* or *"What would you like?"* it was a linguistic symbol of the fact that nobody under any circumstances was prepared to oppress anyone else.

The desire not to oppress either children or adults seems undiminished. It has become part of our shared value system. The fact is that we are living in a materially affluent society and today we have a tendency to follow the illusion that the true focal point is our ability to always get exactly what we want. In other words: if only I am able to do and get everything I want, then I have achieved the optimum life.

We know, of course, that in reality it does not work like that. Every human experience points to other factors that are more important for us if we are to live quality lives. One of these is our ability to set and achieve goals—or achieve at least some of them. Another is our freedom to have, express and live our dreams. To achieve either or both of these we often have to do things and take steps that we do not really feel like. Some of these steps might involve frustration and pain. This applies to our personal lives as well as our ability to contribute constructively to society.

Today's parents will almost constantly ask their children: *"What do you want?"* or *"What would you like?"* they will, to some extent, let children's wishes serve as a guideline. This is more often than not a way for the parents to engage their children's emotions and involve them in family life. In the book *"Here I am! Who are you?—about presence, respect and boundaries between adults and children"* these issues are discussed at greater length. However, some of the highlights are:

- Children are not consciously aware of their needs but will most of the time know exactly what they

want. They need their parents to teach them the difference as they grow older.
- If parents let the children's wants lead the way (out of goodness and love) then the responsibility for the family's well-being is placed with the children. If this continues for a number of years children's sense of empathy and ability to interact socially will suffer. As will the relationship between the parents and children.
- There is no harm in giving children what they want. As long as it does not happen simply because the parents do it to avoid conflicts, gain popularity or suppress their needs and desires.

As the authoritarian family style slowly disappears children are gaining greater freedom. They are invited to make a number of serious decisions regarding their futures. This requires a deep insight into their own lives as well as a developed sense of personal responsibility. There are plenty of reasons to celebrate this development but it does mean that they must have had the opportunity to develop their reflection skills and ability to make decisions. However, we must consider that their parents might not have enjoyed this kind of freedom so their pool of role models is very shallow.

It is therefore a good idea to limit the use of the question: *"What do you want?"* or *"What would you like?"* and replace it with: *"What would you prefer?"* or *"What do you feel like?"*

Smaller children will quickly tell you what they like or do not like and very soon they will also be able to differentiate. Here is an example based on a common conversation—

- "When would you like to do your homework today?"
- "I don't like to do homework!"
- "Alright. Now I know what you don't like. Can you now tell me what you do like."
- "I just told you!"
- "No, you only told me what you didn't like. I understand that you don't like doing homework but are you going to do it anyway?"
- "Yeah . . . I guess, I have to."
- "Yes, if that is what you want to do."

— "I suppose I want to . . . But I don't feel like it.
— "That is alright. You can easily do things even if you don't feel like it."

The child's dislike is taken seriously and he/she is not criticized. Instead he/she will learn something about the difference between likes and dislikes. They are going to need many of these lessons. Sooner or later, and definitely around the age of 10 or 11, they need to be able to make that distinction all by themselves. They will have to select as well as reject some of the options presented to them—perhaps most importantly on the internet. This practice of carrying out an inner dialog between their likes and dislikes gets to the heart of the matter of both children's and adult's self-esteem. Ultimately, it is all about their ability to define their own boundaries in relation to other people, peer pressure, threats and promises.

There is obviously nothing wrong about doing things simply because we happen to feel like it. We just need to be able to do both: make serious choices as well as indulge the moment.

But . . . Children become sad when we say "No!" to what they want most of all. This is true and is first and foremost because of their experiences as infants. During the early years their experiences of love and care were directly linked to having their wishes and needs satisfied as quickly as possible. When parents and others suddenly start saying "No!" they will become sad and frustrated. However, their tears are an important part of the nourishment they need to grow and be able to function in relation to other people. It certainly is not love that makes parents avoid or prevent children's frustrations. It is either sentimentality or an attempt to be seen as a "good" mother or father.

Love must be relevant, otherwise you are only "well meaning". We must give our children what they actually need to be able to live good lives. As challenging as it may seem—this is the reason why saying "No!" is often the most loving answer.

When should we say "No!"?

You obviously need to determine when you want to say "No!" Allow me to present some general considerations and experiences.

Let us begin by looking at the things parents cannot say "No!" to. We must never say "No!" to doing our very best to fulfill our children's fundamental needs for belonging, closeness, safety, food, care, clothes, warmth and sleep. Were we to deny them this we would be guilty of failing in our duty of care and risk losing the right to live with them. There are still parents who for a variety of reasons are unable to live up to this responsibility and have to leave it to others for shorter or longer periods of time—or for good. Inadequate parents are no worse than any other parents, they are just not privileged enough to be able to make it happen.

Apart from that, parents can—technically speaking—say "No!" to whatever they like. Allow me to propose the following reflections before doubt leads you to a definite "No!"

The reflective "No!"

You need to consider your own values, needs and personal boundaries, and relate this to the consequences your "No!" might have on the child's life. From as early as age two or three you are able to include their thoughts, experiences, fears and expectations in your considerations. This does not mean that they are able to make decisions to the same extent as you but it does mean that they have a right to be heard and taken seriously. Their contributions will often be both surprising and valuable. Involving them is an invaluable way for you to stay up to date with their concept of self, their boundaries and desires. Children are not particularly adept at talking about their emotions, nevertheless, when they are given the opportunity to talk about what is on their minds, they are surprising good at expressing themselves.

In today's world we are not left with much of an opportunity to be in doubt and take the time needed to consider things carefully in order for us to make genuine decisions. Although it is worth taking that time to consider things carefully. You will definitely not be a worse parent for it. Often children seem unable to wait for you to make a decision, but when all is said and done, they do respect parents who make an effort to reach the right conclusions.

There are plenty of things that are part of our children's lives which we as parents have little or no regard for. These trends or fads continually change. For years it was Barbie dolls for girls and Pokomon for boys. During other periods of time it might be war toys and soldiers. For some parents this does not present a problem at all. Their children can have whatever is in fashion at any time. No questions asked!

There are no objective arguments or academic research that supports parents either way. You will have to do what you see fit and follow that intuition. It is a good idea to start this process at an early age when the choice is no more challenging than to choose between a box of LEGO or a

Barbie doll. Just ten years will pass before those decisions will be far more difficult and the consequences will be lasting. The important part is that the children grow up in a family where they learn to take themselves and each other seriously.

There is no doubt that children will react when they are being told "No!" They might be disappointed, sad and angry. This has to be taken seriously. We must never criticize, use irony or ridicule their emotional reactions. From their point of view their reactions are both necessary and relevant.

Most children have the ability to cry in eight to ten different ways and it is important to be able to tell the difference. Tears as a result of conflicts with parents are often an expression of their frustration (a mixture of sadness, unfulfilled expectations and anger.) This is a completely normal and necessary reaction that must be expressed before they are able to move on and learn from that experience. There is no reason for you to get upset or feel guilty. There is even less of a reason to feel that you have failed as a parent. Children's frustrations are an issue that parents ought not get involved with. They should neither comfort nor try to bring the frustrations to an end. It might be appropriate with an empathetic and acknowledging comment, such as: *"I did not realize that you wanted it that much!"* or *"I can see that this made you very disappointed. I hope you feel better soon."*

This is exactly what is so challenging and troubles many parents. By acknowledging how much the child wants something they feel they have already given in and think they are obliged to say "Yes!" This is not the case at all. You do not have to comply with the child's wish just because you have asked them—*"What would you like for dinner?"*, *"What would you like to do this Sunday?"* or *"What would you like for Christmas?"* You do not have to give them what they want, just because you ask them. Asking these questions stems from some good democratic values that certainly benefit the children. I often ask my wife what she would like for dinner without being obliged to serve this. Likewise, she might ask me which dress I think she should wear—only for her to return a while later in a completely different one. Questions of this nature show an interest in getting some input, inspiration or perhaps a desire to be challenged. Neither party should feel bound by the answer—irrespective of who asks. Being right or getting things your way might mean that you are taken seriously—but it is only one of several ways of being taken seriously. Sometimes it might also mean that the one who asks does not feel like having a conflict or getting into an argument.

The spontaneous "No!"

I am confident that many parents regularly feel they instantly need to say "No!" when their children want to do something or ask for things. They might have norms or values that are so ingrained that they do not need any consideration at all. This might be something they carry from their own childhood or something rather irrational and very difficult to explain. If this causes a serious conflict it is worthwhile considering our motives but it is not always necessary for you to be able to explain the reasons for the "No!" It is, in fact, more important that the parents are able to stand up for their right to be irrational than that they invent some convoluted pedagogical explanation. For example—

"I can't tell you why I say "No!" because I am not really sure myself. I just know it is what I mean and you will have to accept that for the time being."

Humans are not rational beings and I honestly believe it is very important that adults as well as children stand by their right to be irrational—and even unreasonable. A few days, weeks or months later we might revisit the issue and talk to the other person about it again. Were you to make up some explanation to suit the occasion you might also be blocking your ability to subconsciously work on the issue. You would be none the wiser from the experience.

There is no reason for parents to know the answers to everything. Neither do they have to be reasonable or sensible all the time. Children know perfectly well what it means to be irrational and they do not benefit from being with adults who try to be something they are not. I seriously believe that the right to be unreasonable ought to be written into the UN's *Convention on the Rights of* the Child—or whoever has a suitable mandate. It ought to stipulate that: *"Every child has the right to spend some time with adults who are not pretending to be super-human."*

When "No!" is non-negotiable

Should a "No!" always be negotiable or would that mean that the parents are too indulgent and inconsequent? It should, in fact, always be negotiable as long as two conditions are in place.

The first condition is that the adults do not see their "No!" as so important that it is set in stone. The second condition is that a genuine negotiation can actually take place. This should involve dialog or conversation without nagging, blackmailing or unfair manipulation. If these negative aspects occur then parents must carefully consider what they can do to change this destructive trend.

Negotiations are not just the domain of business people and politicians. It is indeed one of the many ways of expressing equality within the family. It is often through negotiations that we learn more about each other and ourselves. It is also a way for us to gain valuable information we would otherwise not have access to. A parent who after a serious negotiation sticks to the "No!" or turns it to a "Yes!" gains a lot of respect from their children—much more than the parent who is indifferent to other people's opinions.

Is it not important to be consistent, though? That really depends on what is meant by "consistent". If you really mean you must be true to your values and prepared to connect these with your decisions and actions, then it is important to be "consistent". If you however, believe you must have the same opinion today as you did a week ago, then it is not important. That would, in fact, be rather silly, as you would deny yourself the opportunity to learn and check in with reality. This is what living with children is all about—learning more about yourself, your children, your values, your opinions and the decisions you make.

In some families there is a frightening lack of consistency because parents are not prepared to enter into conflicts or because they try to gain short-lived popularity. This makes children feel insecure and their world becomes incoherent.

It also teaches children how to blackmail and manipulate parents.

Often, negotiations are about whether or not the child should be able to fulfill their wishes. It is not important if the negotiations lead to any of them changing their mind. What matters is the quality of the negotiations because this is what determines the nature of their relationship and their perception of the outcomes.

The quality of the negotiations depends on both parties' ability to speak up for themselves and listen to each other. Were they to criticize the other's opinions it would quickly turn into an argument—or a battle for power. No matter how intelligently and civilized this is done, it is no longer a negotiation and it seldom leads to a constructive outcome for anyone involved. It is easy to win and hurtful to loose but loneliness is the only predictable outcome.

Many adults complain that children are such competent negotiators and that the whole process has become too strenuous. This is partly because they have not been prepared to pick up their children's art of negotiation which is very much about being as specific as possible. It is understandable that parents and teachers do not find it meaningful to spend hours negotiating everything and anything. All they need to do then is insist on a break. For example—

> — "I don't want to spend hours talking about this but I do want to know what your opinion is. Why don't we take a break now and bring the issue up again later when both of us have had the opportunity to think things through."

The child's reply will almost certainly be:

> — "But, I . . ."

Then you help them by saying:

> — "I meant what I said. In the meantime you might want to go over your arguments again and make sure you present them in a brief and exact way. In return, I promise to listen very carefully."

Equality and democracy are similar in the way they both take time and require engagement. As a parent it is tempting to wish for a return of the good old days when an adult's word was law and the child's desire to negotiate was considered impertinent or down right rude. This approach is certainly possible with younger children but it comes at a price.

Without a "No!" there is no "Yes!"

Before we take a look at issues related to saying "No!" to older children and teenagers it is important to acknowledge that a prerequisite for saying "No!" is the ability to say "Yes!" with all of your heart.

One of the traits all humans seem to have in common is our need to feel comfortable about saying "No!" before we can say "Yes!" This applies to ourselves and within our family. It is also the case in relation to our friendships, the society, in-laws and employers—in fact, any other human or institution that we value and would like to have a well-balanced relationship with. When we do not experience the freedom to say "No!" and to look after our own individuality we are left with three humiliating options:

1: Replying with an apathetic "Yes!";
2: Telling a lie; or
3: Blindly following someone else's orders.

Children do not hide anything and are sometimes brutally honest. They will say "No!" to some of the things you want of them, such as brushing teeth, getting dressed, going to kindergarten, tidying their room, doing homework or one of the many other things they have to do. When their "No!" is met with criticism, persuasion, motivation, threats or promises both of you will instantly loose your dignity. If you instead were to repeat your request and then give the child some time (often just a few minutes) they will automatically convert their resistance to co-operation. They will be able to say "Yes!" with their personal integrity intact as supposed to blindly following your orders.

While a family can be a very loving and caring community it is also a complex system of power struggles. Every now and then members need to fight for their individuality. This very important mission has a unique password: "No!" The family structure and the parents' leadership determine whether this happens through open and honest confrontation or through guerilla warfare. A community that respects every member's individuality will develop as a strong community. When there is a lack of this respect the result will be either suppression or a strong battle for individualism.

The autonomous child

There are a number of children for whom the option to say "No!" before they say "Yes!" is part of their nature. We call them the "autonomous children" because from birth they have boundaries more precisely defined than most others. There is nothing "wrong" with them, they are just different from other children who prefer to blend in with their parents and willingly let go of their own boundaries in favour of the experience of warmth, care and submission.

We are often, but by no means always, able to recognize this autonomy at birth. From our experiences, their face and body seems more "mature" and they will have little baby fat, their muscular system is well defined and they are often further developed than children of the same age. Behaviorally, they are not influenced by most of what we call care and guidance. They are very uncomfortable to body contact which they have not themselves initiated. They recoil from any kind of adult behavior unless it is 100% authentic and they are immune to pedagogical manipulation. Most show these traits only at home while others also behave like this at childcare and at school.

It is indeed challenging for their parents, as they will often feel inadequate and get the impression that their love is rejected. A highly distressed mother with an eight year old autonomous daughter put it like this: *"I have raised three children without any particular issues but with her I feel that she just doesn't love me. I obviously love her but she doesn't want me or my love—certainly not in any way similar to the others. I can't give her a hug at bedtime and she goes to sleep much later than we think she ought to. All the routines that her other siblings have had, she completely rejects. From the moment she was born and I held her in my arms, her body has felt still. I am not allowed to brush her hair or touch her. Whenever it suits her, she will wear a summer coat in the middle of winter."*

Autonomous children have, in fact, exactly the same need for closeness, care and guidance as any other child, but they will decide when and to what extend this will happen. They will always perceive that other people are struggling between a desire for connectedness and a need for separation. Figuratively speaking, they require a smorgasbord to pick from when other children are very happy to be fed and served. They take their personal boundaries very seriously and only when they have the freedom to choose are they able to say "Yes!" In many ways they behave just like mature, grown up adults with a healthy sense of personal integrity and self-esteem.

As soon as parents learn to be available without being pushy, motivating, lecturing or manipulating the autonomous children will be very accepting and receptive. They become soft—physically speaking—and they express a sense of relief as they escape their loneliness. They will stop rejecting your care only when you are able to wholeheartedly acknowledge their peculiarities.

Saying "No!" to tweens and teenagers

"Tween" is the marketing term for 10 to 13 year olds. It is a contraction of "between"—the years when they are between childhood and puberty. Psychologists call this the pre-pubescent period. As a market segment they are a significant force. Not surprisingly, this has caught the attention of the big marketers who seriously contradict many parents' values. The fact that supermarkets place sweets at children's eye level is nothing to speak of compared to the many commercial inputs that have free access to the minds and bank accounts of tweens.

Add to this the fact that the norms and values that matter most to the tweens become those of their contemporaries rather than those of their parents and family. This does not mean that the parents' values no longer matter. It just means that the tweens need to work out how to maneuver between two sets of values. However, these values often collide. As your children are well into the process of trying to deal with all of this they are suddenly struck by puberty and once again everything is turned upside down. As parents we will be challenged and feel provoked by this upheaval. Yet, it blends into complete insignificance compared to what our children will be going through. The impressions, the manipulations and the transformations that are forced upon them are significantly challenging.

From this moment and onwards the parents ability to exert their power decreases rapidly. Just the thought of digging your heels in and saying "No!" seems as hopeless as it seems necessary. Luckily, you do not have to resort to bans and orders to gain influence.

You must never forget that your values and the way you conduct yourself still plays an important role in their consciousness. It is however, not always easy to detect, as they most likely only will be using their personal language—and the language of their culture. This makes sense when we remember that they have just spent 10 years of their lives adjusting to your views of the world—and have been 100% loyal to this. From now on, things are different. You live in the past and they belong to the future—a future to which the parents will only ever be given a visitors pass. As the children grow older they will use the language of the future and it will be worth trying to interpret what they say, as it will be the language they will use for the rest of their lives.

For this reason alone it is crucial that you continue to represent your own values and accept that opposition is inevitable. You must continue saying "No!" when that is what you believe in—and you must also always support their right to say "No!" Building bridges between the past and the future is important and this is predominantly a responsibility that lies with the parents.

As a parent, it is no doubt difficult to let go of your power and control no matter how delicately and democratically it has been used. Just having the option of issuing bans and orders is very much synonymous with being a responsible parent. In some ways this is true. As we describe below, at certain times it would be irresponsible not using this power—no matter the motivation.

The tween years give parents time to get used to a new type of responsibility and say "Yes!" and "No!" in different ways—less like parents and more like "sparring partners". You must learn to be a partner who offers maximum, yet, relevant opposition and does minimum harm. This will inevitably require more frequent, longer and perhaps more complex negotiations. Some families will also experience much rougher conflicts. How many and how rough depends on how well you have been able to deal with the conflicts that arose during childhood.

When your 13-year-old daughter wants to go to a party with an 18-year-old you can confidently say "No!" if you like—even if one of her girlfriends have been given permission to go. This might result in a bad atmosphere for a few days and she might for the rest of her life recall this as being totally unfair—both of you will just have to live with that.

Should your 15-year-old daughter have a similar wish you ought to do whatever is in your power to influence her final decision but it would be unwise if you were to use your power to prevent her from going or to punish her in anyway. From the beginning of puberty it will be their responsibility to take responsibility for themselves. If you as a parent are a skilled negotiator you might be able to gain some influence on her decisions. But from this point in time she will have to reach her own conclusions based on her own upbringing, her personal experiences and of course her dreams and goals.

Say "No!" and feel comfortable about it when you feel it is the right thing to say. This is the only way you can help them build enough personal integrity and confidence to say "No!" to some of the things you so desperately hope they will say "No!" to—those terrible things the big bad world is trying to tempt them with. You might be accused of living in the dark ages and understanding *"f. . . all!"* but that is not a definitive measure. The important thing is that you are able to live with yourself afterwards.

It might seem pointless to say "No!" if they do whatever they want anyway. Sure, it is pointless if you want things your way all the time. It is important though, because of your relationship and because of your personal peace of mind—it also has a greater impact on them than they will let you know.

In some families the teenage years end up being a time when everyone says "No!" to everyone all the time. Parents continually try to set limits and put up restrictions, and the young ones constantly reject their guidance and direction. If this happens, it is about time for the parents to look at the children they have raised and make the decision to say "Yes!" to the person he or she has become—for better or worse. Opposition and conflicts are indeed natural and perfectly normal interactions during this period of time. Warfare however, is not—especially not if it is constant and goes both ways. It is the parents' responsibility to bring this to an end. You will have to acknowledge that your attempt to guide has failed—no matter how well intended and reasonable it has been. Instead, spend your energy on taking care of the relationship between you and your child. Getting things your way is not what matters. What does matter is you ability to trust each other—and stay in contact.

The issue of trust is really difficult. Historically, we have a long tradition of passing the responsibility for trust and mistrust to the other person.

— "How can I trust you again, when you don't . . ."
— "On a number of occasions you have proven that I can't trust you!"

In actual fact, our trust in other people is *our* emotions, and we are responsible for those. The mistrust often occurs when others do not live up to *our* expectations to how we want them to behave. For tweens and teenagers our trust is everything that matters and when they do not experience it, they are seriously lost. This is why they become so desperate when it fails. It is all about you trusting their best intentions and that they do the best they can with the insight and experiences they have.

During these years they are trying to work out how much of what the parents stand for they themselves are prepared to say "Yes!" and "No!" to. Their intent is not to distance themselves from their parents but to define their personal boundaries, needs, desires and goals. The way in which the parents have been able to define themselves during the previous year will show itself in the way their children say "No!"—inside as well as outside of the home.

Some young people will find their way out of childhood comfortably and with much personal confidence. Others will have to fight their way out of childhood.

The personal "No!"

There is no better "No!" than the personal "No!"—even though it is difficult.

The process of finding this "No!" will be enriching for you. You will show genuine respect for others and make the biggest personal impact possible. Add to this the fact that it is warm and inviting, and you will experience growth in your feeling of self-worth.

Before we take a closer look at the personal "No!" let us consider some ways of saying "No!" that are not personal.

— "No! You ought to be ashamed of yourself!"
— "Who do you think you are?"
— "You simply can't do that!"
— "How could you even consider asking?"

— "You must be out of your mind!"
— "All you do is want, want, want! How about thinking about others for a change?"
— "You know very well what I think about those thing, don't you!"

These examples are possibly aggressive and fairly critical. Now for a few more evasive and vague examples of "No!"

— "It is probably not so good right now, but I am not sure really . . ."
— "I am a bit stressed today so you'll have to wait!"
— "Don't think its because I don't like you, but . . ."
— "Under normal circumstances . . ."
— "Yes, but you'll have to wait till later!"
— "Sure, but then you will have to promise me . . ."

Historically, personal expressions were considered improper. They were seen as embarrassing, presumptuous, pushy or self-centered. No doubt, this was convenient for societies and family structures where our ability to be subordinate was what counted—where the individual's desires and needs did not rank very highly.

In recent times things have improved. The relationships between the genders and between parents and children have certainly allowed for new norms and benchmarks guiding the way families share their time and the way we relate to each other. However, there are still people who bitterly oppose these improvements in human relationships. There is also a growing mass who is trying to come to grips with these new ways of thinking and being—some more successfully than others—but a fast growing group of people nonetheless.

The personal "No!" stems from our personal values, experiences, emotions and personal boundaries. It is essentially motivated by our personal responsibility. The kind of responsibility that puts us in charge of our own emotions, thoughts, actions and choices which we either take on board or ignore. Regardless, we must face this single handedly. The personal "No!" is also the enemy of any authoritarian system, yet, it is absolutely necessary if we are to live in a democratic world and enjoy the benefits of equal relations. Otherwise, we will become each other's victims and burden the community without contributing to it.

The personal "No!" has nothing to do with any kind of rejection. It is all about saying "Yes!" to ourselves. We obviously have to compromise from time to time. But if this involves sacrifice of essential aspects of our inner self then we are not only compromising with others we are also compromising ourselves. Then our personal integrity will suffer which will not only reduce our quality of life but also the quality of our relationships with others. It is however, not such a simple task defining our own values and boundaries, as they are often and easily confused with our opinions and attitudes. When our values are challenged by our nearest and dearest it often turns out that our values cannot stand this challenge. More often than not, we will find that we have stumbled upon some of these quite randomly. If this is indeed the case then our values will need to be revised and refreshed, otherwise they end up being a kind of shield which only has one function, namely to protect us from those who are different to us.

This does not mean we must always tread cautiously out of fear for offending others. It is very important that our family and friends feel comfortable sharing their wishes, desires and needs with us. They must also feel supported in their efforts to fulfill theirs. This is how we know when to say "Yes!" and when we have to say "No!"

Regrettably, our "self" is not one of those fixed measures we can ever fully get a grip on. Our "self" evolves and matures as time passes and depending on the various relationships we have. Ironically, the more the core of who we are is being challenged the easier it is for us to know who we are. It is through these challenges we continually define and redefine our "self".

When you are watching TV and your five-year-old son thinks you really should be playing with him instead, you will have to make up your mind. Either you say "Yes!" because you prefer to play with him or you say "No!" because you prefer to watch TV.

— "No Paul, I don't want to play with you right now."
— "Why not?"
— "Because I prefer to watch TV until the News has finished."
— "But . . . Don't you want to play with me?"

— "No, not right now!"
— "You are dumb if you don't want to play with me."
— "Yes, I can see how you would think that. But today, that's the way I am."

Some might think that this is an unacceptable response as the poor boy might feel rejected. To "feel rejected" is a psychological way of describing a child's experience when their parents are constantly emotionally inaccessible. A common consequence is that the child feels rejected every time someone says "No!" to them. In the example above the boy is not pushed away by an insensitive parent but he receives a warm and friendly message saying that the parent does not want to play until after the News. He might get angry and feel disappointed but there is nothing wrong with that. However, things would go wrong if the message was impersonal such as in this example—

— "No! Can't you see I am watching TV!"
— "Why don't you want to play?"
— "I have just told you. Go to your mother!"
— "But . . . Don't you want to play with me?"

— "I have just said "No!" Be quiet! I can't hear anything!"

Many parents probably dislike this interchange because it might bring back memories. Therefore they prefer to opt for the following middle ground approach—

— "Not right now, darling. Dad just wants to watch the News. It won't be long."
— "But . . . Don't you want to play with me?"
— "Yes, of course dad wants to play with you but don't you think you could play on your own just for 10 minutes? Then you are a sweetheart and I'll come and play."
— "But . . . Why do you only want to watch TV?"
— "I don't watch that much TV!"
— "But . . . You have to play with me right NOW!"
— "Can't you let me relax for a little while longer, then I'll play with you. Maybe you can find a book so we can pick a bedtime story for when you have to go to bed . . . All right, what do you want to play?"

This example is likely to end in a mess because of the half-hearted messages conveyed by the father. Neither father nor son received what they wanted or needed. The son became frustrated because he was not able to connect properly. The father became frustrated because he sacrificed himself without being rewarded with a grateful and happy son. Frustrated children cannot develop harmoniously, and frustrated parents are always in defensive mode and will constantly feel guilty.

The satisfaction and dignity that comes from the ability to look after yourself and accepting another person's right to do likewise, is exactly what makes the personal "No!" so warm and rewarding.

When we respond to children with a personal "No!" they will soon learn to respect other people's needs and boundaries. There is little they would rather do than to co-operate with their parents and they are fully capable of respecting them. If you instead implement rules and boundaries or make reference to age differences and traditions they will test the validity of these—over and over again. Knowing that both parents believe in what they say and say what they believe in is one of the most valuable and long lasting presents we can ever give our children.

The male and the female "No!"

When our son was around three years old he would come to the desk where I was working. He was curious and wanted to join me so he pulled my trouser leg to get my attention. I asked him to wait while I quickly tidied my desk so the most important papers would survive his desire to explore. As soon as he sat on my lap he would say: "*Me write!*" and grabbed a pen and paper. After a while I needed to get back to work and told him so, put him back on the floor and turned my full attention to the work I was busy doing. More often than not, he would be happy and walk away. At times he did not think he had had enough of my attention and go and find his mother's lap somewhere else in our house.

When his mother sat at her desk and the same situation occurred he would immediately get her attention. She did not take the time to remove what she was working on and as a result she often had to rewrite a few pages of her work. After a little while she would gently hint that she was really busy and unfortunately had to continue working. He on the other hand happily continued what he was doing. When she finally put him on the floor, he was unhappy and would cling to her leg. If I was around she would end up blaming me and claiming that I never looked after him—a simple issue of saying "Yes!" and "No!" had turned into a regular drama.

This is a typical situation and probably sounds familiar to most parents. Many men are simply better at saying a "No!" that cannot be misunderstood. I have met numerous couples where the mother had plenty of stories about conflicts with the children when she was alone with them, whereas the father seldom had similar issues when he was alone with them. Instead of learning from each others' experiences the situations often ended with accusations about being too indulgent and inconsequential or too insensitive and rigid.

The male "No!"—or the definitive "No!" does not belong to men and fathers only. There are plenty of mothers who learn to master it too. It is difficult to define the difference between the genders. Perhaps part of the explanation simply lies in the fact that historically women have had limited opportunities to say "Yes!" to themselves, compared to men who have been able to do what they wanted—at least within the family environment.

Nevertheless, it is certain that many mothers (and their children) would benefit from letting go of their sense of guilt and negative conscience. Guilt and negativity send vague messages and force children into constant confrontations simply because they have not been given clear messages.

Lately, some fathers have been infected by feelings of guilt and have become scared of confrontations with their partners as well as with their children. There is nothing wrong about seeking consensus and being considerate. Howver, it is not very wise to become self-effacing in an effort to gain some domestic peace.

Many fathers are not aware of what it is that they are more capable of than most mothers. They often think it is a simple issue of the two having different attitudes to raising their shared children. This is why men cannot support their wives or partners in their efforts to develop better relationships with their children. This is unfortunate, as many women would benefit from active support, more inspiration and positive help to take better care of themselves. It would indeed benefit the whole family, but it is easier to sit back and be critical.

Saying "No!" to your partner

We should never forget the importance of saying "Yes!" to each other. Following that, one of the best things we can do for our partners is to help them say "No!"

Not many of us are able to do this by ourselves. This is why we need support, help and the permission to say "No!"

— "How about we visit my sister and her family this weekend?"
— "Has she called?"
— "No, but it is a long time since we have seen them!"

— "Well . . . I had actually thought that we could . . ."
— "Think about how often they visit us. We always have a great time."
— "Sure, that's true. But it isn't that long ago we saw them last."
— "Why do you never want to do the things I suggest—or the things I want to do with my family?"
— "I am not saying that I don't want to. It is just that . . . Okay then, let's do it."

As soon as this couple has had a number of these discussions the only possible outcomes are emotionally destroying allegations and a very negative atmosphere. We might be able to blame the woman for manipulating and the man for being weak but that does not serve anyone any good. Here is a healthier version:

— "How about we visit my sister and her family this weekend?"
— "Has she called?"
— "No, but it is a long time since we have seen them?"
— "Well . . . I had actually thought that we could . . ."

— "I would like to but it sounds like you would prefer to do something else."
— "No but . . ."
— "What would you prefer?"
— "I would really prefer to have a quiet weekend at home."
— "Its alright for you to say "No!" to my suggestions."
— "But won't you get angry then . . . ?"
— "I might! But that is not anywhere near as dangerous as if you don't say what you really mean. I would like to see my sister but I also want a husband I can trust. As soon as I know where you stand I am able to sort out the rest."

This time the woman did the best she could. Instead of spending the weekend being responsible for having made a decision for her husband, she gave it back to him. This was not an attack but an invitation to join a constructive conversation.

There is nothing wrong with taking each other into consideration and looking after each other. But in the long run it will seriously damage the relationship if the partners are not able to look after themselves. When you are part of a relationship it is no longer "my problem"—it is "our problem" because the responsibility you are not willing to take ends up being your partner's—and this will be an extra heavy burden.

It might seem easy for fathers to say "No!" to their children and it might seem difficult to say "No!" to their partners. There are plenty of reasons for this contrast—and some rather pitiful ones too. Let us consider the consequences of the unspoken "No!":

- Your partner's trust in you will decline, no matter how genuine your intentions are.
- The intimacy will slowly decrease as the unspoken "No!" becomes more and more frequent. They build up in your system and will eventually surface as aggression or defense. The many seemingly insignificant ways of saying "No!" will join forces and become an important and definite "No!" to your relationship.
- The unspoken "No!" will grind on your self-respect and thereby on your feeling of self-worth.

- You are not being a good role model for your children.

You might wonder how much all of this really matters because nobody is perfect and people work out how to live with each other anyway. This is true. It is also up to you how you choose to live and how you will get on with things.

Children obviously have a general need for living with the best possible role models. History—and all our research—tells us that boys in particular benefit from growing up with a father who is able to (and brave enough to) say "Yes!" to himself and "No!" to his partner. Girls have the same need but in general they look at their mothers who have become much better at standing up for themselves in relation to their husbands. Add to this that girls often go through a period of time when they say "No!" to their mothers in order to work out how much or how little they are alike.

Boys still lag behind girls when it comes to finding their mental and emotional adulthood. This is partly due to the fact that mothers have a tendency to service and overprotect their sons. This is also due to sons not learning to say "No!" to their mothers. As boys will not be like their mothers there is no reason for boys to try to distinguish themselves from their mothers. Boys are dependent on having good masculine role models—men who are big enough to say "No!" to the women they love when their integrity or boundaries are challenged.

The art of saying "No!" to your adult partner and good friends does not differ from the art of saying "No!" to your children. It is fundamentally based on your personal ability and willingness to say "Yes!" to yourself and feeling okay about it. Many of us must start by saying "Yes!" to ourselves and wait patiently for the good feelings to work their way through the layers of guilt, negative conscience and the fear of losing. These layers might be as hard as the crust of the earth.

You have every right to say "Yes!" and "No!" whenever it suits you—but you will have to claim that right. It will not be presented to you on a silver tray.